Spell Jars for Beginners

The Modern Witch Compendium. 56 Magic Recipes to Fulfill All Your Wishes (2022 Guide for All)

Zelene Graves

TABLE OF CONTENTS

A LITTLE BACKGROUND

Witch bottles have been around since the 1500s and have typically been used to resist spells, bad spirits, and magical assaults. These containers are now utilized for a variety of applications and are sometimes referred to as "spell jars." Some researchers believe that the origins of witch bottles may be traced back to Elizabethan England, particularly Anglia, where superstitions and belief in witches were prevalent, and where they were also known as "Bartmann" or "Bellarmine." The latter is owing to Cardinal Bellarmine's bottles, a particularly terrible Catholic inquisitor. These pots were up to 9 inches tall, had a round belly, were made of dark or grey clay, and were adorned with grim bearded faces meant to fend against evil, house spirits, bewitch targets, and erase curses or hexes.

Bellarmine bottles were also used to hold some droplets of blood and offerings to the spirit that resided inside them. When they were in use, they were usually buried or concealed behind a protective ridge in gardens, walls, chimneys, and thresholds.

Because of the immense power, they managed to hold in them, these jugs were highly durable and popular among the witches of England. Even though its most well-known term is a parody of the cardinal's opposition to the Reformation, these types of bottles were not always known as "Bellarmines." Originally, they were made in a German colony named Frechen.

They were known as Bartmann jars in Germany, which translates as "bearded man" jars due to the bearded visage that usually featured on their side.

The witch bottle custom was brought to America by colonists after it became popular in England in 1660, owing to the witch hunts. A witch bottle is mentioned for the first time in Joseph Glanvill's "Evidence on Witches and Apparitions." An unbroken jar was discovered in Greenwich (England) in 2009, and scientists have dated it to the 17th century. Overall, historians believe that the inventors of this witch bottle had to be European immigrants (or their descendants) who had learned folk magic techniques associated with the Old World and sought to reflect the concentration of many catalysts and forces in a tiny container.

However, the Greenwich bottle was not the only one discovered. So far, eight witch bottles have been unearthed in the United States, the oldest of which is known as the Essington Witch Bottle from Pennsylvania.

This jar was discovered during an excavation on Tinicum Island in the Delaware River in 1976. It was discovered upside down and buried on the side of a property, containing urine and pins. What was its purpose? It was said to have been buried to preserve the surrounding area and the people who lived in it. What about the feces? Urine is a historical habit that denotes "marking the territory," as we shall discuss in more detail later in this book.

Another motive for the inclusion of such fluids (still present in certain jars today, along with sperm and menstrual blood) is to "connect" or "join" the purpose of the bottle with

5

the owner of the goods contained inside it. In other words, utilizing the owner's urine ensured that the bottle's aim was uniquely tied to its inventor and not to be combined with anybody else. The Essington witch bottle is said to have been made in the 17th or 18th century when urinary ailments were widespread. So it might also have been a means for the jar's creator to seek protection from such diseases.

Later, during the American Civil War, a fad of similar charm bottles to fight against evil arose. These folk magic objects were most often found in locations where Civil War troops stayed, slept, and recuperated. They were almost certainly employed to keep the ghosts of the dead at bay.

The building of bottle trees, like the American Civil War and European spirit jars, began in the 9th century in Central Africa as a manner of expelling bad spirits who had been caught in the bottles when they ventured too near to the tree. This habit was also carried to the United States by individuals transported to the nation to serve as slaves. They are still manufactured and utilized in the Southern and Greater Appalachian areas of the United States.

However, amulet bottles are also manufactured in South and Central America. They include written prayers, herbs, miniature icons, and talismans that are used to invoke saints and spirits for assistance. These jars are usually filled with holy oils and are always kept on the practitioner's altar.

Furthermore, the usage of magic jars in the conjuring of the Black and African diaspora, as well as Hoodoo folk rituals, is still practiced today. Moreover, although being associated with old magic, the popularity of these bottle spells has expanded among practitioners of a variety of contemporary approaches as well. Many Wiccan and Wiccan-influenced practitioners, for example, use spell jars in their magic.

Overall, myths and traditions concerning certain witch bottles have been handed down through centuries, altered or somewhat adjusted. As a result, they provide us with distinct variants and traditions based on old magic and its most current developments.

Nowadays, you can discover potters and artists that create modern copies of these lovely ancient bottles, and you can even have your jar painted, carved, or engraved.

However, the availability and diversity of materials used for bottling, canning, and preserving are considerably greater now, which means that modern witches do not have to use just brown earthenware. Of course, the longer the material lasts, the better.

Glass is by far the most common option these days, however, it is not always the strongest.

WHAT PRECISELY ARE SPELL JARS?

These little glass bottles sealed with candle wax and covered with a cork or lid symbolize a magical weapon used for protection, breaking a curse, or repelling negative energies and magical assaults. They are also known as bottled spells or witch's jars.

As previously stated, in ancient times, they were generally filled with items such as old rusty nails, razor blades, shards of glass, urine, and other substances with unique properties and enormous magical strength, known as catalysts in the Craft.

They were buried or concealed near the maker's house to absorb the bad powers that were sent to them. This is why, a few centuries ago, it was quite usual for a family to bury a bottle on their land for plenty and protection.

People who are afraid of being cursed may choose to toss their jar into the fire, knowing that when the bottle explodes, the enchantment is broken. In other words, in many folk traditions, these charms were utilized as a type of protection or "counter magic," a method of preventing and capturing the negative effects of witchcraft.

However, magic jars may be used to create curses as well as defend against them. In that scenario, urine, hair, or nail clippings from the victim (rather than the manufacturer) were put in the bottle along with threads to resemble "traps." Other

8

substances that were regularly utilized were saltwater, earth, sand, stones, knotted ropes, feathers, shells, plants, flowers, salt, oil, or ashes. Also present were rusty nails, thorns, glass, wood, and bone fragments.

Instead of casting a curse, modern witches have started to use bottles for charms of protection.

As a result, a magic jar is a today regarded as a weapon expressly intended to counteract any negative.

Overall, it is utilized as a protective aspect of the house since its presence annuls bad spells, psychic assaults, enemy plots, unfair competition, enmity, friends with double standards, or cruel family members.

It is also indicated for protection against misfortune, accidents, falls, and sickness. In other words, it acts as a negative energy absorbent sponge, absorbing any potentially hazardous element.

Because of their tremendous efficiency, the most popular witch bottles are those meant for protection. At the same time, magic jars are created to attract love, money, and prosperity, among other things.

Modern witches usually put particular materials inside the jar to fit their aim. A witch who wishes to attract love, for example, may fill her bottle with red wine, lavender buds, apple slices, and rose quartz. Then, after casting a spell on the bottle, she may leave it in her bedroom to attract the lover of her dreams. Similarly, a bottle may be put in the room of someone who is unwell in order to absorb their ailment. Its contents are thereafter thrown out and buried to spread it.

As previously said, once produced, the bottle should be buried in the garden of the home. However, many individuals today prefer to put it someplace secure at home, leave it in their purse, or spill its contents into a river or sea to flow, to mention a few options.

Overall, there are as many sorts of bottles as there are individuals who manufacture them, whether you want to attract riches, happiness, friendship, job, health, protection, intuition, or love.

And, by combining plants and materials that are precisely suited to the task at hand, you may develop a very powerful instrument to help you achieve all of your goals.

Important facts about spells

So, are you fascinated and eager to learn how to make a magic jar that can help you achieve your goals?

This is fantastic, and I really feel that magic jars may help you improve your life in the same manner that they improved mine. But, in order to use all of their power in the best and most ethical manner possible, you need to be aware of a few fundamental notions regarding spells if you are new to this kind of magic.

As you may be aware, casting a spell entails engaging in a ritual in which you must use your intentions, energy, and spiritual power to achieve the specific goals you want.

A spell may be cast by anybody, regardless of gender, age, studies, or career.

Spellcraft, like other divination methods, is founded on the concept that inside each human is an entire cosmology that represents the scope of the universe: the microcosm stands in for the macrocosm.

Spellcasting is fundamentally the act of finding, raising, and directing your energy. It does not need anyone faith, rule book, aptitude, or privilege. In truth, the only necessary instrument is one's own magical purpose.

This is due to the fact that items and rituals are only conduits for a person's inner power: they are not inherently magical; they simply aid in the channeling of human energy. The tools and materials you use in your spell jars and spells will be determined by the sort of magic you wish to do as well as what you are most comfortable with.

Remember that when you first start out in the art of magic and spell jars, you won't need to invest in a vast collection of costly and exotic materials.

Instead, you'll be able to get started with ingredients that are almost certainly already in your kitchens, such as sugar, salt, cinnamon, black pepper, rosemary, and basil. By adding a few colored candles, paper, and ribbons to this combination, you'll have a very strong beginning kit.

In general, the most important rule of spells is that they should never be cast with malice or with the goal to harm yourself or others. The karmic basis of magic is the law of threefold return: whatever energy you direct will be returned to you with three times the force. Also, if you are undecided whether or not to perform a specific spell, don't. Your magical intentions define your soul, therefore nourish it with love and compassion at all times.

The key to effectively casting a spell is to focus your thoughts on what you want to achieve and to focus your mind on the correct pictures and words. This implies that you must have a good attitude throughout the magic jar building process in order to achieve your goals and avoid being sidetracked by anything else. After all, when you cast a spell, you are performing a rite that will cause a shift in your life's trajectory.

HOW TO CONSTRUCT A SPELL JAR

It is now time to discuss the ingredients that should be included in your magical witch bottle.

First and foremost, they should be things that are relevant to the person or circumstance you are aiming to influence. Generally, the contents of these jars are selected for their recognized utility or based on how the things connect to a circumstance or activity. This associated purpose and the significance of the things inside your bottle are referred to as a "correspondence" by witches. When dealing with "folk magic," correspondences are the same thread that weaves various spells. The majority of correspondences are drawn from history, tales, or folklore and might be symbolic, sympathetic, or therapeutic.

Everyone has their own style of doing magic, as well as preferences and procedures for what to do right away.

It is also critical to recognize that each magical tradition has its own set of methods, applications, and conventions.

In any event, before proceeding, I believe it is critical to state that a witch bottle is merely a container. The form may be anything you want it to be. The fact that these jars are tiny and simple to conceal is a frequent feature, so keep the size of the bottle you want to use in mind. Although you may come across several recommendations online, keep in mind that witches in ancient times worked with what they had on hand. As a result, don't waste too much time hunting for "the right bottle": an empty (perhaps dark) tinted glass container with a maximum capacity of 8.5 fl oz will do for your own jar.

It's not the look that's important; it's the power it carries.

Let's go through all of the steps you'll need to follow to make your own magic jar.

Just bear in mind that these are general suggestions to help you make your own bottle. The most essential thing, as I often say, is that you follow your instincts in every magical performance you do.

So, before you begin performing the magic, you must ritually cleanse and purify your place (e.g., sweep it with your art broom). Then, carefully collect all of the ingredients that will be used in the magic. I also recommend that you form a protective circle before beginning and call on your guides, guardians, and ancestors for added strength and power.

Next, define the purpose of your bottle and what you want to accomplish with it. It might be a magic jar for protection or plenty, for example. If you want protection, you must be extremely precise about what you desire and mean by that. Physical protection, for example, is not the same as magical protection. And there are other types of plenty that you may ask for. So, the very first step is to restrict your objective.

Obviously, you'll need a bottle with you. Small bottles, as previously said, are preferable. Jars of one fl oz and above may be used, but 8.5 fl oz is a good size.

In general, I recommend keeping it as small as feasible. Why? You will need fewer supplies if you choose a smaller vessel. You won't have to "waste" herbs and crystals by building anything larger than necessary.

However, while selecting a container, bear in account your assembly preferences, materials, and the location of your magic jar. If you wish to utilize stones, for example, I recommend choosing a container with a larger opening. If you want to conceal or transport your witch bottle, you should choose a jar that is particularly tiny.

If you want to build a protection spell, on the other hand, you should definitely opt for something a bit larger in order to hold a significant number of components.

If you want to bury your jar, choosing a biodegradable one is a great way to preserve Mother Nature.

If you don't want the components of your bottle to be visible, use anything in amber, blue, or another opaque color.

Before using your jar, be sure to thoroughly clean it by hand-washing it and then set it on a prepared baking pan (newspaper may also be used as a liner). Then, bake it for around 15 minutes at a low temperature in your oven before allowing it to cool. As an alternative, clean the bottle with sunshine or incense smoke. You may opt to wash the lid as well, but you don't have to bake it.

Following that, as previously said, you should research which correspondences are suitable to utilize for your specific spell. What day, time, moon phase, plants, minerals, and deities are most relevant to the reason you seek? If you're new to this and don't know anything about correspondences, don't worry: we'll go over them in-depth in the next pages of this book!

Once you've determined what you may utilize, you must ensure that you have all of the necessary elements. My advice is to concentrate on ingredients that are easy to get and readily available in your location and at that time of year. If you need mistletoe but it is not in season or weather, you should look for an alternative. Any words of wisdom? I like to use dried herbs to have a broad range of plants accessible throughout the year.

You should also think about the personal part of your magic jar. What exactly do I mean? If it's for you, you may want to incorporate some of yourself into it. Hair, fingernails, or even personal fluids such as perspiration, saliva, blood, urine, and so on.

At the same time, you may fill the bottle with a picture of the person or object that you wish to keep OUT of your life. It might be a phobia, a vice, or even a threat. Filling the bottle with unpleasant and especially repulsive materials indicating repulsion and expulsion might also make sense: it's up to you and the kind of magic you wish to do.

Overall, as previously said, bear in mind that you do not need to collect sophisticated parts.

Dry herbs, leaves, flowers, and grains, as well as stones and crystals, are readily available and may be used in practically any kind of spell.

Money spells work best with coins or cash, whereas sugar and honey work well for attracting items. Hair, photographs, nails, and even blood are often utilized to connect your magic to a specific individual. Confetti and glitter assist you in both celebrating and receiving love. Vinegar and urine, on the other hand, are very effective in keeping someone away, protecting, and cleansing.

The most crucial thing is that you constantly pay attention to the connection of each piece. For example, if you want to make a balance spell jar, you should gather herbs and reagents that match your goal (such as salt, sea, coriander, and so on) and use yellow, or a comparable tone, for candles since yellow is regarded to be the color of balance.

So, to give you a sense of how this works, let's look at some of the most prevalent connections of this kind below.

Petite cardamom pods or powdered cardamom, carnation petals, cinnamon sticks or ground cinnamon, coriander seeds, hibiscus flowers, linden flowers, mint, rose petals, weeping willow leaves, ginger, orange tree blossoms, saffron, red wine, or bark

For good luck, use ash leaves, bay leaves, cumin seeds or powder, dill seeds or leaves, whole or crushed nutmeg, and vanilla pods.

Cedar chips or shavings, fir needles, marigold petals, marjoram, orange peel, oregano, savory

Peace basil, catnip, lavender, lemongrass, olive twigs or leaves, rosemary, violets, violets, violets, violets, violets, violets, violets, violets, violets, violets, violets, violets, violets,

Acorns for prosperity, allspice, almonds, dried banana, cloves, oak leaves, oats, poppy seeds, rice, saffron threads, sage

Protection angelica, black beans, cactus needles, garlic powder or garlic salt, nettles, crushed black pepper or black peppercorns, thistles, rose hips, black salt, vinegar, rusty nails, hyssop, rosemary, rue, dragon's blood, pine needles, nails, pins, sea salt, tobacco, or a black candle stamp.

Caraway seeds, eucalyptus leaves, ginger, pine needles, rose hips, sunflower petals or seeds, thyme, cedar, dill, fennel, rosemary, and vinegar are all beneficial.

Also, keep in mind that a substance or object having a link to your persona or true significance for you will function much better than one purchased in a store.

The petals of your bouquet, for example, are much more potent than those of the flowers you gathered on your way home. I'm not saying the latter won't work; I'm simply suggesting that you choose things that are relevant to you wherever feasible.

Please keep your objective in mind and concentrate on what you're doing when assembling your materials. What exactly do I mean? That you should not clean the home or take phone calls when cooking your jar!

After you've determined the objective and acquired the materials, you may bless your items and jar and continue with the ritual you like before doing your magic, such as a cleaning bath. Next, with a clear and concentrated mind, prepare your bottle by considering how each item or ingredient will help you get closer to your objective, and light one or more candles whose hue corresponds to your purpose.

To prepare your jar, carefully calculate the proportions of your materials and keep in mind that there must be visible layers of each one in the jar, so don't combine them.

Personally, I recommend that you begin by adding a coating of coarse salt to your bottle. I do this with the majority of my jars in order to bless, protect, and cleanse the target of the spell.

However, if your magic necessitates the usage of a symbol or token, include it first.

This will help you keep focused on your task from the start. A sign of this kind is often a personal object stolen from the spell's victim.

As previously said, a strand of hair, a piece of cloth from a garment, or a photograph. However, anything as basic as the person's name scribbled on a sheet of paper or inside a paper bag can suffice.

Then, again, add your dry materials depending on the many correspondences and your goal: carefully consider what you want your spell to perform and the best method to represent it. Personally, I prefer to start with a layer of crystals, then two or three herbs, and then another layer of crystals.

You may then pour moist stuff if you desire. These may include various kinds of spelled and blessed waters, oils, and alcoholic drinks like wine, vodka, or rum. As previously said, classic witch bottles discovered in Europe included urine: it is entirely up to you whether or not to include this kind of fluid, as well as, for example, blood. Vinegar and honey are also typical liquids in Hoodoo spell jars, and we'll go over them in more depth in just a few lines. In any event, it is widely assumed that negative energy may be drowned in liquids.

Of course, you may continue the historic practice by including sharp things such as shattered glass, pins, tacks, or knives.

Each time you add a new layer of ingredients to your bottle, you may choose to speak a blessing, prayer, thought, or purpose. You will enable the strength of your request to focus better by doing so.

When all of the components are inside, leave just enough room for some air and the stopper to seal so that the herbs, salt, and other ingredients may settle in. Also, leaving some space at the top will enable you to shake the contents of your jar to respond to it (if you want to, of course!).

After that, secure the cap with a liberal coating of candle wax to ensure that the jar is entirely airtight. For more sophisticated spells, you may give your jar a little additional power by putting a similar ribbon around it or writing something on it.

Finally, you must activate your witch bottle; this entails to put your purpose in action and do the "casting" How are you able to accomplish so? In a variety of methods.

You may shake the bottle, anoint it with oil, perform incantations, or place a candle on top of the jar and let it burn down (only make sure the cork bottle stopper doesn't catch fire!). You may also opt to burn the whole candle at once or to light it a little bit each night during the waning or waxing moon phases. Again, it is totally dependent on your particular tastes.

And you may always devise a technique that you believe is more powerful and suited for your particular spell.

When your witch bottle is finished, I recommend holding it in your hands for a few moments and meditating with it. You will be able to connect with the power of your jar in this manner: I really feel fairly good after this quick meditation time!

WHERE SHOULD YOU KEEP YOUR MAGIC JAR?

You should store your bottle in one of two places, depending on its use. And maybe it should be a gloomy one. A healing bottle, for example, maybe placed in the ill person's room, a love jar beneath your bed, and so on.

You may either set it on your altar to continue working with its enchantment or put it in your freezer to freeze anything you don't want to happen.

If you want to bury a protective or defensive jar, you may do it in your yard, garden, or at a crossroads. The buried bottle represents Mother Earth's protecting function, which is capable of instantly dampening any bad energy.

On the other hand, the rationale for placing it at a crossroads is because many people see this hallowed transitional region as a place of enchantment and mystery.

The origins of such a notion may be traced back to ancient Greece when the Greeks thought that the crossroads signified and symbolized the union of forces (mystical and invisible).

But it was also the balance of opposites, and it was a point where time and space met, making it ideal for transformation and development.

You may also opt to toss your jar into rushing water or let it sink in the middle of a lake or the sea: just keep in mind (I know, I say it all the time, but Mother Nature is much too important!) that legally this is littering. It's not too awful to do it a few times a year, but don't overdo it. Also, bear in mind that you should bury or submerge your jar if you don't want to undo any spells.

Last but not least, one of my personal favorites: you may choose to bring your magic jar with you.

Yes, you are correct. You may carry the bottle in your luggage and let its charm follow you everywhere you go (just remember to keep it hidden from others!).

To me, it's as though my one-time spell transforms into a charm or talisman that I may keep near for as long as I choose. And I believe this is simply incredible.

Anyway, remember that this is YOUR witch bottle, and as long as you keep it secure, it will work for YOU. So, always listen to your instincts, and if you feel the need to move your bottle or add another thing, do so and be free to let the magic flow.

The only need is that you never open it since all of the defensive ingredients are contained in it.

The bottle's expiry date is determined by the fulfillment of the objective; you should not discard it until it has not been accomplished or you detect a persuasive advancement.

And how long does it have an effect? If it does not have a set date, you may elect to replace it every six months to renew its energies and abilities.

The reality is that witch vials may endure for hundreds of years.

When properly prepared, summoned, and sealed, their influence may last a lifetime! Actually, over time, the components in the container may "move" or "change form," and you may even see pictures in them. If this occurs, it indicates that the bottle is in good functioning order.

So don't be astonished if you see its efficacy.

Just keep in mind that, depending on the contents, they might occasionally explode or become... well, unpleasant. In this instance, you may opt to discard your jar and recast the spell with a new one.

24

What if you unintentionally open your witch bottle?

The reality is, that you shouldn't do anything like that until the spell has produced the desired consequences. In any event, if you break your jar and your spell, you shouldn't be too concerned. Simply examine what function the spell served and, based on that, determine if you need to replicate it right away or not.

I'm also often asked whether it's feasible to use an old witch bottle for a new spell. Despite my strong belief in recycling and helping Mother Nature, I would not advise it in this circumstance. Especially if you want to cast a love spell in a jar that was previously used to repel negativity. Why? Because you can never be certain of the quantity of leftover energy that may still be there.

This is why I recommend having many bottles on hand: you can buy them at practically any kind of store (remember, they don't have to be costly!) Alternatively, you may cast your spells in a pickle, spaghetti, or salsa jars. If you still want to utilize old ones, fill them with soil from your backyard, garden, or any other natural area near your home, and then bury them in the same location for a few months. The earth and its components will then remove any lingering energy from your previous spell, allowing you to utilize it again.

Is it possible to reverse a spell?

It is, indeed. You may take the jar apart and return the natural things (herbs, rocks, and so on) to Mother Nature. If your bottle includes crystals, you will need to clean and disinfect them thoroughly and gently after they are removed from the container. Depending on the purpose of the spell, you should either bury the contents of the jar or dump them in a river or another natural body of water (as long as this is not unlawful, of course!).

Also, please double-check if these ingredients are natural and biodegradable to avoid harming the environment. If you wish to reuse the bottle for a fresh spell, rinse it out with moon water, waft the smoke of burning sage about and within it, lay it on a windowsill beneath the full moon or in the sun, or fill it with earth and bury it as previously stated.

If you don't want to retain the jar, you may light a fire (again, as long as it's legal and you're not endangering anybody) and toss the whole bottle and its contents in it. Fire is a symbol of destruction, and it was formerly the most frequent method of dispelling spells and curses.

Overall, remember to keep your witch bottle hidden at all times. As the saying goes, power shared is power lost. So, to keep your spell's potential, don't tell anybody about it.

Also, bear in mind that spell jars, in general, are like being fed. What exactly do I mean? That you may choose to light a fresh candle on the top of your bottle from time to time to refocus on your objective. You may do this every day, every week, every month, or whenever you feel like it. Simply ensure that the hue of your candle matches the original spell, and consider this option ahead of time since you will not be able to activate a magic jar that has been buried or thrown in a lake.

In any event, keep in mind that spells might take some time to perform their magic, depending on your goal. This implies they aren't immediate, and you should be prepared to wait rather than become disappointed if you don't obtain what you want in a matter of hours.

Magic takes some effort on your part. You can't create a love spell and never leave the home, expecting your better half to appear in front of your door. You'll have to go out, meet people, chat with them, and perhaps risk expressing your emotions. Similarly, constructing a money magic jar will not automatically lead you to a billionaire lifestyle if you don't even attempt to discover money-making chances or hunt for a job.

Spells do not guarantee certain outcomes, but rather improve the likelihood that what you wish will occur. As a result, if you cast a spell to achieve something that has a 0% probability of occurring, you must understand that no magic will make things better. However, if you are attempting to earn a promotion and are working hard and putting in additional hours every day, employing a spell jar will boost your chances of getting picked among the many contenders. In summary, the Universe encourages us to work for what we desire.

Last but not least, keep in mind that occasionally the Universe's response to a certain question will always be "no." And no spell, no matter how strong, will ever be able to alter it.

Spells with a honey jar and a vinegar bottle

I'd like to say a few things more regarding honey jar and vinegar bottle spells. Why? We may argue that they represent two different extremities of the magical spectrum within the same family of rituals.

Honey jar spells, also known as sweetening jar spells, are one of the most talked-about types of container spells in current practice, both locally and globally. In general, they are used to manipulate a circumstance or a person to the practitioner's advantage.

The fundamental aim behind this kind of magic is to transform a certain circumstance by sweetening it.

So, for example, they may be used to help you get something from someone (this might be anything: a dress, a new job, or even a divorce!); or to make someone be kinder to you and treat you the way you deserve.

They indicate a vast variety of possibilities, as you can see, and you may use them to cast love spells, friendship spells, job spells, and so on. In addition to honey, they may be made using many types of syrup, sugar, sweeteners, and molasses.

On the other hand, vinegar bottle spells are available. They are employed to sour a situation, as you may have surmised, by using the opposite method of dealing with an issue. Overall, they are used to turn someone's case against them, to put impediments in their path, cause difficulties, promote strife, and even do destructive magic. They are also known as break-up spells, even though, as we have seen, they may be used for a variety of purposes other than breaking up couples.

Honey jar and vinegar bottle spells are regarded to be more versatile in their applications since they are part of a live folk magical tradition that has consistently grown and evolved on their roots throughout time.

Correspondences in magic

As promised, let's now concentrate on the most crucial types of correspondences to consider while designing and constructing your magic jars.

Correspondences are ties between the ethereal and the physical, which you may create using the instruments you employ to cast your spell, the time you pick to perform it, and many other factors.

To provide an example, if you want to cast a love spell, it is ideal to do it on a Friday, Venus's day, and with a pink candle, the color of love.

Assume you are already a correspondence specialist. In such a case, you may simply skip this section and move right to the chapter on the actual production of various magic jars.

If you are a novice, I recommend that you read the next pages once without attempting to remember all of the various associations, and then keep this guide close at hand to refer to the future pages whenever you need to reference the magical characteristics of a certain element.

In any case, let's start with the moon phases, one of the most potent instruments you have at your disposal to greatly improve the magical outcomes of your spells.

Phases of the Moon

So, how can you know which moon phase is best for performing or creating a certain magic jar? Let's have a look at it right now.

Phase 1: New Moon

The new Moon ushers in a new cycle. The Moon is rarely visible during this phase, and the sky is mostly dark. With the Moon veiled, you are in an excellent position to identify your dark parts, which you generally want to keep buried.

For example, you may have a manipulative side that you deny exists until someone points it out to you. There are always healthy ways to employ those specific skills, and New Moons are the ideal time to figure out how to make them operate constructively.

Also, since Fresh Moons represent new beginnings, this is an excellent time to create goals and intentions for the upcoming cycle. Is there anything specific you'd want to see happen in the next 30 days? Is there a toxic partner you're finally ready to let go of to create a place for the one you've always wanted? The New Moon, on the other hand, represents your opportunity to start again, particularly in love. So, if you're ready to let go of the past and attract the ideal relationship for you, this Moon phase provides you with an excellent chance.

This phase's spells and rituals may be performed from the day of the new Moon until the three days following it.

This phase is white in hue.

The following are some subjects to focus on during this phase:

Any new undertaking or activity

 Relationships and love

Setting goals and objectives

Health, beauty, and self-care

Job search

Fresh starts

Phase 2: Waxing Crescent Moon

The waxing crescent Moon phase occurs when the Moon transitions from a New Moon to a Full Moon and becomes visually more prominent and dazzling. During this period, the Moon increases brighten, and offers an excellent environment for sympathetic magic centered on growth. What exactly is sympathetic magic? The one that employs symbolic resemblance. Because the Moon is shining brightly, you must harness that energy to make your profession, self-esteem, and love life shine brighter as well.

This phase's spells and rituals may be performed three and a half to seven days following the new Moon.

This phase is white in hue.

Examples of subjects to focus on during this period include:

 Emotions

Business and work

Changes and new beginnings

Projects and ideas

Amulets and other magical instruments preparation

Creatures

Phase 3: The First Quarter

This is the phase of the Moon when we can see half of it. And the luminous region of the Moon becomes bigger and larger as the days pass. It's a great moment to start building and the perfect time to set the groundwork for something sturdy and long-lasting. If there are elements of your life that you are unable to organize or that are not functioning as you would like, this Moon will provide you with a fresh chance if you apply yourself and make an effort. So make use of all of your equipment and magical resources.

This phase's spells and rituals may be performed seven to 10 days following the new Moon.

This phase is white in hue.

Examples of issues to focus on during this period include:

Health

Luck

Motivation in general

Personal connections and friends

Inner strength and bravery

Phase 4: Waxing Gibbous Moon

This phase occurs when the Moon is more than half full and the illuminated surface of the Moon continues to grow. The name "gibbous" is of Latin origin and means "hump," a term that has been used for ages to describe circular formations.

The gibbous Moon phase is an ideal moment to make significant and long-overdue adjustments. Don't be alarmed if you perform a spell that doesn't seem to have the expected effect. Sometimes a gestation period is required, and no impact is instantly noticeable during this time. So make use of this time to unwind and prepare any additional magical rituals you wish to undertake, taking advantage of the energy of the forthcoming full Moon.

This phase's spells and rituals may be performed between ten and a half and fourteen days following the new Moon.

This phase is red in hue.

The following are some topics to focus on during this phase:

Love and Romance

Dreams

Creative pursuits

Spirituality

Patience

Inspiration

Phase 5: Full Moon

When the Moon is full, emotions flow strong, and everything becomes much more intense. You may utilize its potency and apply it to almost any spell you wish, knowing that you can rely on all of the Moon's power to assist you. You may also charge your crystals during full Moons by putting them in an area that is directly exposed to lunar light. Another method is to create Moon Water by placing a cup of water beneath its glow.

In other words, you may do any magic with increased potency during the full Moon, having in mind that this is also a period when psychic talents are enhanced.

The spells and rituals of this phase may be performed fourteen to seventeen and a half days following the New Moon.

This phase is red in hue.

The following are some topics to focus on during this period (although the Full Moon is ideal for almost any form of magical ritual):

Finances and employment

Love and romance

Dreams

Family connections

Fertility

Safety

Phase 6: Waning Gibbous

The waning gibbous phase is when the Moon darkens again, transitioning from a full Moon to a New Moon. In general, now is the time to let go of everything that keeps you adversely connected, such as harmful habits or addictions.

The declining Moon may help you break links with a former partner, and it is also a great time to rid yourself of bad emotions such as uncertainty and insecurity.

This phase's spells and rituals may be performed three and a half to seven days following the Full Moon.

This phase is purple or black in hue.

Examples of concerns to address during this period include:

Stress

Emotions

Addictions of various types

Difficult choices

Divorces and separations

Doubts and anxieties

Phase 7: Final Quarter

This lunar phase corresponds to the days when the Moon can be seen in the sky during dawn and morning, and it is distinguished by the fact that half of the Moon is lighted while the other half is not. The northern hemisphere's left side is gleaming, whereas the converse is true for the southern hemisphere.

The last quarter phase is an excellent time to expel the negativity that surrounds you and to continue the task of exile that you began before.

This phase's spells and rituals may be performed seven to ten and a half days following the full Moon.

This phase is purple or black in hue.

The following are some subjects to focus on during this phase:

- Rest

- Isolation

- Adversity

- Addictions of every sort

- Difficult choices

- Concerns and insecurities

Phase 8: Waning Crescent

This is the final visible phase of the lunar cycle, and it is the time to concentrate on self-care and relaxation to recover all available energy for the next one. It is also important to acknowledge your goals and dreams and to nurture your connection with the divine and spiritual as much as possible.

So, what are you going to do? First and foremost, use the energy of this Moon to practice forgiveness and self-compassion to heal your inner scars. This phase also promotes relaxation and allows essential information to be gleaned from dreams and the unconscious.

As far as possible, you should have a relaxed and reflective approach, avoiding starting new initiatives or engaging in new and dangerous behaviors.

This phase is purple or black in hue.

The following are some subjects to focus on during this phase:

Healing

Relaxation

Spirituality

Self-Care

Forgiveness

Purification

Phase 9: Dark or Black Moon

This phase lasts around two to three days and the Moon is not visible in the sky at all.

This is also an excellent time to get rid of items in your life that you no longer need, while also reflecting on what you have already done and what you want to achieve in the future.

It is best to begin dealing with any form of opponent at this time.

This is also a good time to take care of oneself and find comfort in solitude.

The spells and rituals of this phase may be conducted while keeping in mind that the dark Moon appears once every 32 months and can last anywhere from one and a half to three and a half days.

This phase's color is (of course!) black.

The following are some subjects to focus on during this phase:

Opponents

Obstacles

Achievements

Things to Avoid

Cleanliness

Self-Care

THE SEVEN DAYS OF THE WEEK

The day of the week on which the spell will be performed is one of the many factors to consider while creating a magic jar. Each day of the week is connected with a certain planet (among them, the Moon) and is associated with masculine or feminine energy, a God or a Goddess, earth elements, stones and crystals, and so on.

So, while casting a spell, it's also a good idea to seek the magical day of the week with the traits that will help your efforts the most.

Yet, bear in mind that the day of the week does not have the same significance as the phases of the Moon; however, if you can match the appropriate day with the most favorable lunar phase, you will be able to construct an even more potent witch bottle and boost your chances of success.

In any case, if you've been waiting for months and everything else is great, don't put off preparing your spell jar because the day of the week doesn't appear to be the best: your magic has a higher purpose that will make the day you cast your spell wind up being right for YOU.

With this in mind, let's take a look at the seven days of the week's primary magical correspondences:

Sunday

Name Origin: The Sun

Planet: The Sun

Energy: Male

Deities: Brigid, Ra, Apollo, and Helios

Colors: Gold and Yellow

Crystals: Topaz, Sunstone, Amber, Quartz, Diamond, Carnelian,

Tiger Eye

Herbs: Marigold, Sunflower, Cinnamon, St. John's Wort, Incense

Associations: Success, Prosperity, Fame, Strength, Wealth,

Promotion, Miracles, Healing

Monday

Origin of the name: The Moon

Planet: The Moon

Energy: Feminine

Deities: Moon, Artemis, Diana, Selena, and Thoth

Colors: White, Silver, Pearl, Light Blue, Light Gray

Crystals: Moonstone, Opal, Aquamarine, Pearl, Selenite

Herbs: Willow, Lotus, Chamomile, Catnip, Peppermint, Sage,

Comfrey

Associations: Intuition, Fertility, Dream, Dreaming, Illusion, Femininity, Peace, Spirituality, Justice

Tuesday

Name origin: Germanic God Tyr

Planet: Mars

Energy: Masculine

Deities: Tyr, Mars, Morrighan, Tiwaz, Lilith, Aries

Colors: Red, Pink, Orange, Black

Crystals: Bloodstone, Rhodonite Flint, Garnet, Ruby, Rhodonite

Herbs: Holly, Basil, Cactus, Thistles

Associations: War, Courage, Rebellion, Protection, Conflict, Success, Strength,

Wednesday

Name origin: Odin's Day (Woden)

Planet: Mercury

Energy: Masculine

Deities: Woden, Mercury, Hermes, Athena Lady Fortuna, Odin, Lugh

Colors: Yellow, Magenta, Orange, Purple

Crystals: Agate, Citrine, Aventurine

Herbs: Lilies, Lavender, Eucalyptus, Fern, Aspen, Aspen

Associations: Business, Arts, Chance, Transportation, Wisdom, Healing, Communication, Creativity, Fortune, Debt, Contracts, Music, Education

Thursday

Name origin: Thor

Planet: Jupiter

Energy: Masculine

Deities: Thor, Zeus, Jupiter, Juno

Colors: Royal Blue, Green, Purple

Crystals: Lapis Lazuli, Lepidolite, Sugilite, Amethyst, Turquoise

Herbs: Oak, Clove, Sage, Honeysuckle, Lemon Balm

Associations: Honor, Wealth, Abundance, Loyalty, Business, Travel, Education, Healing, Harvest, Prosperity

Friday

Name origin: Frigga

Planet: Venus

Energy: Feminine

Deities: Freya, Venus, Aphrodite

Colors: Pink, Gray, White, Water

Crystals: Jade, Lapis Lazuli, Coral, Malachite, Coral, Rose Quartz,

Emerald

Herbs: Feverfew, Cardamom, Saffron, Apple Blossom, Strawberry

Associations: Love, Romance, Friendship, Covenants, Grace,

Balance, Prosperity, Passion, Fertility, Birth, Pregnancy

Saturday

Origin of the name: The God Saturn

Planet: Saturn

Energy: Masculine

Deities: Hecate, Saturn

Colors: Black, Grey, Red, Dark Purple

Crystals: Obsidian, Jet, Serpentine, Hematite, Apache Teardrop

Herbs: Cypress, Black Poppy Seeds, Mullein, Thyme

Associations - Wisdom, Banishment, Psychic Attack, Self Discipline

Candle Mysticism

Candles, as you are surely aware, are an essential component of any magical arsenal. They enhance and release energy, maybe kept about the home (unlit, of course!) to generate good feelings, and are used in rituals and spells.

Candles have traditionally been used as strong and adaptable magical implements in witchcraft. They may be used alone or in combination with other instruments and substances in spells and rituals.

Candles produce helpful, calming, and soothing energies whether utilized for magical purposes or in daily life.

Candles, in general, signify colors in spells and ceremonies. Each hue has its own set of magical abilities as well as spiritual implications. If your spell calls for a candle but you don't have one in the correct hue, you may use a natural beeswax candle or a white candle and include the needed tone in another way. You may also add essential oil with the qualities of the hue in question to your candle.

Ideally, you should have a range of various colored candles in your toolbox, with correspondences that include, but are not limited to, the following:

White: fosters tranquility and calm while also increasing inner strength and understanding.

Black is used for spiritual protection.

Green: aids in the realization of your ideas and increases wealth.

Blue: interacts with your chakras as well as any emotional traumas that need to be healed.

Yellow: improves social skills and attracts new job prospects.

Red encourages love, sex, and passion.

Pink: increases both romantic and self-love.

Purple: increases spiritual awareness and creativity.

Orange: encourages ambition and bravery while also assisting you in broadening your horizons.

Brown: aids in all aspects of your resources, including health, energy, belongings, pets, and so on.

Gold is a magnet for money, business possibilities, and wealth.

When working a magic jar (or any other kind of spell) using a candle, remember to always use a fresh one. Otherwise, you risk interfering with its power with the aims of your earlier spell work.

Stones and crystals

Crystals are extremely important magical instruments because they may focus and guide energy towards a certain aim. They are even said to have healing properties, both mentally and physically.

45

All crystals have an incredible quantity of magical characteristics, and the objective of the following list is to provide you with a summary of the key ones for each stone to reference before constructing your witch bottle.

Remember that you may add crystals and stones in any form and quantity to your magic jars. Crystal chips, in my opinion, are a terrific alternative because of their small size, which makes them ideal for use in a bottle.

So, let's go through a list of the primary magical powers of some of the most often used gems, which are normally available in real and online shops. Just keep in mind that the items mentioned below are by no means an exhaustive list of all those utilized in magic.

Agate represents acceptance, gratitude, balance, suffering, connection to the Earth, honesty, optimism, pure love, protection, shyness, soothing, truthfulness, quiet, communication, comfort, confidence, bravery, depression, emotional calming, general healing, and generosity of spirit.

Alexandrite: Astral projection and travel; lucid dreaming; tranquillity; psychic balance; regeneration; renewal; rebirth; spiritual transformation; fulfillment; creative powers; eloquence; emotional balance; grace; happiness; harmony; imagination; intuition

Clairvoyance, psychic clarity and visions; self-esteem; sincerity; spiritual communications; trust; truthfulness; divination; eloquent communication; emotional balance, healing, development, and stability; grounding; honesty; inspiration; intuition

Amber represents balance, tranquility, clarity, confidence, bravery, patience, prosperity, psychic protection, purification, victory, wisdom, harmony, knowledge, longevity, meditation, memory improvement, and past-life recall.

Anger release, calmness, concentration, depression relief, intuition, meditation, mental awareness and clarity, peace of mind, pleasant dreams, positivity, pure love, new beginnings and focus, stress relief, communication with deities, emotional balance and calming, happiness, harmony, healing, negative energy, relaxation, spiritual awareness

Astral projection and travel; aura balancing; self-confidence; concentration; focus; intellectual clarity and stimulation are all benefits of amethrin.

Acceptance; mental clarity; negativity removal; self-improvement; shyness; strength; concentration; focus; intellect; intelligence; logic.

Aquamarine: Enhanced affection; meditation; peace of mind; relief from phobias; relaxation; serenity; increased tolerance; authority; calmness; cleaning; closure; compassion; clearing confusion; courage; inspiration; tranquillity; water travel; wisdom.

Aventurine is associated with plenty, adventure, anger reduction, lovelessness, righteousness, prosperity, self-sufficiency, anxiety, equilibrium, banishment, tranquility, professional achievement, harmony, and travel safety.

47

Azurite is associated with challenges, cleansing, emotional empowerment, mindfulness, overcoming barriers, patience, perspective, transformation, truthfulness, facing anxieties, intuition, compassion, mental development, honesty, insight, and life transformations.

Acceptance; heavenly direction; humility; mental equilibrium; awareness; confidence; bravery; decision making are all characteristics of Beryl.

Bloodstone: Adaptability; aggressiveness and anger release; expulsion of hostile spirits and destructive energies; mental balance; obstacles; spiritual alignment and balance; concentration; trust; bravery; decision making; healing and emotional strength; fears; focus; concentration

Acceptance; joy; courage; emotional stability, warmth, and well-being; family communication; connection to Earth; fear release; self-esteem; shyness; sociability; spiritual rebirth; happiness; harmony; individuality; inspiration; compassion; meditation; memory recall; recollection of former incarnations

Celestine: Communication, enlightenment; mental balance; motivation; heart purity; self-awareness; spiritual growth; projection and astral travel; tranquillity; increased communication; compassion; emotional clarity, stability, and understanding; empathy.

Citrine is associated with abundance, achievement, money, nightmare prevention, pleasure, prosperity, psychic protection, self-confidence, self-discipline, success, warmth, willpower, awareness, balance, banishing and repelling negative energy, change, creativity, generosity, mental growth and stimulation.

Quartz is associated with activation, beginnings, cleaning, emotional and mental awakening and balance, concentration, meditation, mental clarity, banishing and repelling bad energies, past-life recollection, psychic clarity, attracting romantic love, self-awareness, and vigor.

Diamond represents challenges, clarity, honesty, hope, justice, longevity, protection, purity, self-confidence, overall strength, dependability, truthfulness, knowledge, bravery, perseverance, faith, and faithfulness.

Compassion; emotional balance and comfort; meditation; relationship healing; self-esteem; stress reduction; dignity; emotional expression; forgiveness; karmic balance and healing; letting go of the past are all characteristics of Dioptase.

Affirmation magic, awareness, concentration, bravery, creativity, emotional balance, persistence, protection, resilience, self-esteem, self-improvement, wisdom, healing and strength, resilience, focus, forgiveness, homing, justice, movement, fresh beginnings, perception.

Clairvoyance; enchantment; faith; fidelity; happiness; protection from evil spell; honesty; insight; intelligence; repel negative thoughts; romance; serenity; development of sixth sense; truthful communication; intuition; joy; knowledge; love; loyalty; remembrance of the past; omens; prophecy; psychic ability; psychic healing and protection

49

Fluorite is used for astral projection and travel, intuition, lucid dreaming, psychic protection, purification, aura cleaning, balance, clarity, divination, dream recall, connection to the Earth, and healing.

Garnet: Balance, tranquility, determination, passion, past-life recall, romantic love, sensuality, social status and success, virility, desire, dream recall, emotional and physical intimacy, stamina, mental and physical energy, nightmare avoidance.

Adaptability; emotional and psychic balance and healing; gardening; optimism; protection; relaxation; dependability; trust difficulties; agriculture; anxiety; balance; boundary establishing; tranquility; focus; connection to Earth and nature

Abundance; calmness; emotional balance; fertility; friendship; gardening; psychic protection; self-acceptance; self-sufficiency; attraction and communication with spirit; wealth; wisdom; good luck; harmony; healing; kindness; longevity; lucid dreaming; mental clarity and stability; release of negative thoughts; new beginnings; peace of mind; tranquillity; practicality; pregnancy; prosperity; protection; psychic dreams

Jasper is associated with: comfort, compassion, relaxation, tranquillity, transitions, contentment, organizational improvement, healing, nightmare avoidance, bad mood, and peace of mind.

Lapis Lazuli: Self-awareness; self-confidence; self-esteem; spirituality; tranquillity; truthfulness; clairvoyance; peacefulness; emotional release; harmony; honesty; intuition; karmic balance and healing; meditation; negativity release; openness; psychic ability, strength, and visions.

Moldavite is associated with beginnings, blessings, meditation, cleansing, transformation, channeling healing energies, consecrations, introspection, and magical and psychic connection.

Morganite: Anxiety; calmness; compassion; emotional healing and health; fidelity; friendship; gentleness; communication, peace of mind; tranquility; self-confidence; self-esteem; pain; spiritual growth and renewal; stress; true love; guidance, love, and magic of the Goddess and God; pain; happiness; heartbreak; infidelity; loyalty; meditation; patience; peace

Moonstone (white): Realization, lucid dreaming, magical strength, new beginnings, prophecy, protection, relaxation, sensitivity, soothing, spiritual communications, wisdom, affection, awareness, serenity, change, divination, divination, full moon magic, happiness, hope, humanitarian love, intuition

Moonstone (gray): Balance; psychic awareness and protection; relaxation; self-awareness; self-confidence; sensitivity; calming; spiritual communications; wisdom; calm; divination; emotional balance and stability; fears; growth; hope; intuition; lucid dreams; magical strength; state of mind; new beginnings; prophecy

Affection; motherhood; fresh beginnings; new love attraction; nurturing; pregnancy; calming; birthing; divine connection and love; emotions; fertility; happiness; hope; expectation; motherly love

Balance; past-life healing; realistic expectations and thoughts; stress alleviation; tension release; bondage; bondage; catharsis; death; disappointment; emotional protection; grounding; inner development; mental clarity; difficulties

Onyx is associated with anxiety, authority, psychic protection, self-confidence, self-control, self-defense, endurance, strength, vigor, bonding, blessings, clairvoyance, consecration, courage, divination, concentration, memory enhancement, mental balance and connection to Earth, nightmares, and past life recall.

Opal is associated with adaptability, previous life recall, tranquillity, psychic skills, romantic love, spontaneity, clairvoyance, early life memories, emotional balance and expression, charm, faithfulness, hope, insight, recollections, and passion.

Blessings, clarity, transformation, truthfulness, trustworthiness, wisdom, consecration, dignity, emotional balance, integrity, love, loyalty, lucid dreaming, moon magic, tranquillity, protection, purification, purity, sincerity, fertility, faithfulness, concentration, gentleness, honesty, inner beauty

Peridot is associated with balance, quiet, relaxation, renewal, relaxing, stress reduction, change, comfort, growth, healing, intuition, new beginnings, peace of mind, self-protection, rebirth, and rejuvenation.

Pyrite improves concentration, mental skills and strength, practicality, vigor, willpower, creativity, deceit detection, focus, objectives, intellect, logical and analytical thinking, memory and recall.

Rhodochrosite is associated with compassion, kindness, tolerance, friendship, harmony, and humility.

Soothing; compassion; self-assurance; self-esteem; calming; tactfulness; civility; emotional balance forgiveness.

Ruby represents balance, fertility, nightmare avoidance, psychic dreams, virility, passion, romantic and passionate love, and protection against psychic assaults.

Selenite: Awareness, balance, judgment, mental clarity and flexibility, psychic healing and protection, elimination of stagnant energy, study, blocking outside influences, quiet, cleansing, clear confusion, decision making, deep meditation, concentration, and harmony.

Adaptability; tranquility; psychic ability; self-acceptance; self-awareness; self-confidence; self-esteem; sincerity; wisdom; communication; emotional balance; divination; fear; honesty; intuition; knowledge; meditation; mental clarity

Clairvoyance; bravery; creativity; mental clarity; psychic powers; willpower; protection from curses; deceit prevention; emotional strength; connection to Earth; wholeness

Topaz is associated with concentration, comprehension, alleviation from sadness and low mood, emotional balance and healing, happiness, honesty, research, and truthfulness.

Tourmaline: Concentration; home protection; mental shield; connection to Earth; protection from Black Magic.

Turquoise: Emotional healing; calm; negative energy neutralization.

Sapphire is associated with balance, focus, memory, clarity of mind and thinking, optimism, relaxation, wisdom, inner peace, inspiration, intuition, and meditation.

Plants, herbs, seeds, and spices

Plants and herbs, and their magical uses, have been used in rituals of protection, purification, prosperity, and love for generations, and it has now reached our day.

Scott Douglas Cunningham (1956 - 1993), a well-known writer and practitioner of natural magic and author of various works on Wicca and witchcraft, extensively discussed the power of the plant life in his well-known work "Encyclopedia of Magical Herbs."

Sage, basil, rosemary, thyme, lavender, laurel, and rue are a few common herbs that anybody may cultivate in pots and then use in spell jars to benefit from their magical properties.

So, once again, let's look at a list of the most often used herbs, plants, seeds, and spices, keeping in mind that those mentioned below are by no means all of those utilized in magic.

Allspice: Success; compassion; courage; efficiency; good luck; job interview success; spiritual, emotional, and psychic healing; repel bad energy; success; winning job competitions; winning in general; efficiency at work; happiness at work

Anise: Divination; fertility; cleaning; legal concerns; love; psychic awareness; psychic shield; protection; nightmare protection; purifying

Basil: Abundance; aphrodisiacs; attraction; balance; banishment; business; calming; clairvoyance; communications; concentration; dissipation; divination; emotional strength; fertility; financial gain; concentration; friendship; good luck; harmony; home protection; honesty; intimacy; libido; mental clarity; money; passion; tranquillity; prosperity; protection; purification; romantic love; self-discipline; sensuality; endurance;

Bay Leaf: Banishment; business; clairvoyance; confusion; curse removal; lucid dreaming; meditation; money; negative energy dissipation; positive energy attraction; prophesy; psychic ability; purification; success; triumph.

Black Pepper: Banishment; binding; purification of the home; protection of the home; repulsion; separation; protection.

55

Borage is associated with attracting business, boldness, creative inspiration, strength, psychic ability, and protection.

Caraway: Soothing; illness prevention; infidelity; meditation; repellant; stress relief

Cardamom: Aphrodisiacs, courage, finances, financial gain, strength, friendship, good luck, libido, love, mental clarity, money, persuasiveness, prosperity, sensuality, sexual love

Catnip is used for animal magic, appearance, attraction, beauty, enhancement, friendship, happiness, pleasure, and love.

Cayenne: banishing; spell-breaking; libido; desire; expelling negative energy; negativity; passion; sexual love; spell reversal; temperament; protection

Centaury: Drive away and repel negative or evil energies, people, and spirits. *Chamomile: Anxiety; calming; children's spells; curse-breaking; divination; emotional protection; happiness; healing; health; spell breaking; lucid dreaming; repelling magic; meditation; nightmare prevention; peace of mind; tranquillity; psychic protection; relaxation; calm; deep sleep; spiritual clarity; stress relief.

Chervil: Ascension to the afterlife; communion with the divine; creativity; inspiration; mental stimulation; past-life recollection; spiritual refreshment; spiritual communications.

Chicory: Making decisions; melancholy; happiness; joy; and uncertainty. Sensuality; sexual stamina; virility; libido; desire; aphrodisiacs; passion

Chives: habit breaking; mental stimulation; positive

Cilantro: aphrodisiacs; attraction; awareness; communication; creative success; creativity; encouragement; imagination; intelligence; libido; lust; mental sharpness; mental clarity; passion; sexual desire

Cinnamon is associated with attracting attention, business acumen, business success, creativity, financial gain, fire magic, intellectual stimulation, libido, desire, knowledge, money, power, prosperity, love, success, and winning.

Cumin is associated with fidelity, desire, love, binding, peace, exorcism, protection from evil, serenity, and tranquillity.

Cloves are associated with achievement, comfort, persuasion, creativity, curse removal, debt payback, encouraging action, perceptions, prosperity, protection, security, financial success, intellectual stimulation, money, and commercial success.

Dill weed: Children's healing; love; barrier elimination; passion; positivism; kid protection; sensuality.

Eucalyptus: Healing, protection, cleaning, purification, spiritual development, and warding off evil.

Fennel is associated with communication, confidence, bravery, earth magic, emotional strength, female fertility, financial ingenuity, fortitude, grounding, mental clarity, motherhood, passion, repulsion, sexual desire, and stamina.

Gaerlic: Protection against accidents, bad and good luck, disease, jealousy, male fertility, negativity, physical, psychological, and sleep protection.

Ginger: Balance, commitment, desire, lust, grounding, healing, invigoration, inspiration, good luck, nightmare prevention, optimism, protection, self-defense, sexual and physical energy, endurance, and stimulation.

Gingko Biloba: Aphrodisiacs; chastity; vigilance; influence; intelligence; longevity; order; character strength; tranquillity; virtue.

Aphrodisiacs, sexual stamina, vigor, and bodily healing are among benefits of ginseng.

Horseradish benefits include fertility, male sexual stamina, protection, sexual enjoyment, and virility.

Anger; anxiety; balance; calm; cleansing; concentration; courage; depression; dissipation of negative energies; emotional balance, healing, and protection; fidelity; concentration; friendship; grounding; happiness; harmony; lovelessness; joy; insomnia; inspiration; lover attraction; loyalty; magical ability; magical power; mental clarity; nourishment; peace of mind; psychological healing; purification; romantic love; calming; stress reduction; unrequited love;

Laurel: Divination, inspiration, healing, knowledge, banishment, protection, and binding

Lemon balm: antiseptic, repellant, and stress reliever.

Clairvoyance, emotional clarity, intelligence, intuition, understanding, mental sharpness, precognition, psychic skills, sensuality, sexual exploration, and studiousness are all characteristics of Lemongrass.

Lovage: Intelligence; establishing a new connection; soul mate attraction

Marjoram: Depression; emotional strength; family happiness; family love; sadness; low mood; death transition.

Mint: Adversity, appetite suppression, tranquility, clarity, creativity, fears, pain, happiness, healing, jealousy, desire, meditation, mental acuity, protection, purity, relationship healing, renewal, repel bad energies and spirits, sexual stamina, pain.

Mistletoe is associated with love, protection, reconciliation, forgiveness, fertility, and sexual potency.

Mhyrr's powers include banishing, breaking curses and hexes, purifying, and protection from mental and magical assaults.

Mugwort is used for aphrodisiacs, astral projection and travel, banishment, blessing, clairvoyance, clarity, consecration, divination, fertility, love, lucid dreaming, repelling negative energies and spirits, prophecy, prophetic dreams, protection, psychic abilities, purification, spirituality, spiritual communications, and truth.

Mustard is associated with acceptance, alertness, awareness, bravery, emotional strength, fortitude, and memory improvement.

Nutmeg is associated with good fortune, intuition, money, and success, as well as winning games and lotteries.

Oregano is associated with astral travel, pleasure, and good health.

Banishment; soothing restless spirits; cleaning; dissipation; fertility; spiritual contacts; spiritual rebirth; honesty

Emotional discomfort; fear reduction; faithfulness; friendship; physical and psychological suffering; self-acceptance; self-esteem; inspiration; longevity

White pepper represents bravery, emotional strength, fortitude, health, self-confidence, and honesty.

Rosemary: Blocking harmful spells; breaking negative spells; clairvoyance; cleaning; clearing; dispelling; divination; healing; intelligence; love; memory; mental clarity; mental energy; preventing nightmares; protection; purification; improving school grades; study abilities

Rue is associated with healing, attracting good fortune, creativity, protection, and psychic growth.

Balance; good fortune; honesty; grounding; longevity; mental clarity; overcoming problems; truthfulness; wisdom

Sandalwood is associated with protection, optimism, the eradication of bad energy, desires, and exorcism.

Fertility, healing, creativity, success, money, passion, desire, and luck are all associated with sesame.

Calming, meditation, memory, mental clarity, psychological healing, relaxation, and stress reduction are all benefits of spearmint.

Confusion; memory; mental sharpness and clarity are all benefits of summer savory.

Sweet woodruff is associated with: balance, change, evasion, garden magic, growth, male fertility, money, prosperity, protection, success, and riches.

Tarragon: Self-assurance; self-esteem

Thyme is associated with awareness, cleaning, attention, focus, insight, memory, psychic healing, purification, spiritual regeneration, and understanding.

Turmeric is used for altar consecration, banishing, binding, privacy, cleansing, secrets, spiritual strength, and instrument consecration.

Recipes for Spell Jar

Now it's time to get down to business with this book. We'll look at some of my favorite magic jars on the following pages. As you can see, it is a highly wide assortment, drawn from several traditions and aimed at providing a magical answer to a variety of issues and circumstances. Some of these witch bottle suggestions are incredibly simple to make: they only take a few ingredients and, in my experience, don't even require you to chant your spell aloud to be successful. Others, on the other hand, suggest utilizing more ingredients and doing a little more additional effort on your behalf. You may prepare all of them or just a few of them, always attempting to begin with the simpler ones to get acquainted with this specific magical practice.

I won't say it again, but remember that the precise amounts of the ingredients are up to you and are primarily determined by the size of your bottle. Similarly, remember to always light your candles before the ceremony starts and to do any rituals that you believe are more suited for your magic and aim.

As I previously said, I have opted to be completely upfront with you, revealing precisely how I do things and even giving you alternative solutions to the same issue. But, as I will never tire of emphasizing, YOU are the most important component of your magic.

So, if you have a feeling that a certain item or term isn't going to work in your situation, don't be afraid to trust your instincts. Make the adjustments that seem right in your heart, and believe that your spell will assist you in achieving your goals. Because if you believe it, it will come true.

Last but not least, a little curiosity before we begin. Do you know why this book has 56 spell recipes?

This number, on the other hand, carries the energy of the numbers 5 and 6, making it one of the most optimistic and strong.

It brings with it adaptability and ingenuity, two crucial characteristics for success in life and issue solving. You should not doubt that the Universe has supplied you with all of the essential resources you need to achieve your life objectives. However, things don't always go as planned, and this is when you have to be creative and find a method, no matter what, to make your goals come true. And what greater assistance could there be than knowledge of strong magic jars?

In other words, this is my present to you to help you find your way through the dark days that never seem to end... I have a feeling you'll achieve fantastic things with it!

Spell Jars for Protection

1. Protection spell jar (option 1)

You will need the following things to build this protective magic bottle:

Any size glass bottle with a cork

Dried or fresh rosemary

Needles

Pins

Red wine

Black candle

Fill your jar halfway with dry materials while saying aloud the following or similar phrases: " "ails, needles, rosemary, wine; the power is mine in this bottle.

Keep me safe from danger and hostility; this is my choice, so be it!" "

Imagine these components performing precisely what you just stated.

Fill the jar halfway with dry ingredients, then pour the red wine, leaving space for a little air. Cap the bottle and seal it with some wax from the black candle. Bury it in the furthest corner of your yard and draw the pentagram (five-pointed star) above it.

2. Protection spell jar (option 2)

To build this protection spell jar, you will need the following ingredients:

A glass container of any size with a cork

Three teaspoons of coarse salt

Cactus thorns

Iron nails or spikes

Cotton knotted thread

A few pieces of shattered glass

Basil

Sage *Sandalwood

Vinegar A blue candle

Take three sections of a long line and entangle them so that the bad energy stumbles with the thread

A few pieces of broken glass

Basil

Sage

Sandalwood

Vinegar

A blue candle

Fill your bottle halfway with each item, leaving some space for air. Meanwhile, speak the following or similar things aloud: " "Each ingredient is potent; each component is intended to assist me.

Please keep me safe now and forever.

Thank you. Thank you, thank you, thank you."

Then, lid the jar and drizzle some candle wax over the top to seal it. Then, on a piece of paper, design a symbol of protection, such as a rune or talisman, that reflects the kind of protection you need and attach it outside your bottle.

Hide it at the entrance of your house to keep malevolent desires, ill-intentioned or negative energy away from you or your property.

3. Spell jar for protection (option 3)

You will need the following things to build this magical bottle to attract protection:

A glass bottle with a stopper of any size

Sea salt

Sewing needles or pins

Nine rose thorns

Mustard seeds

Mint

Mistletoe

Red wine

A white candle

Fill your bottle halfway with each item, leaving some space for air. Meanwhile, say aloud or something close to "Thorns and needles, salt and seeds, Protect my house, and so be it!"

To seal the jar, cap it and drizzle some candle wax over the top.

Place it at the entrance to your property or in a well-hidden location at a crossroads.

4. Spell jar for protection (option 4)

You will need the following ingredients to make this magic bottle to attract protection:

A glass bottle with a stopper of any size

Ash

Brown sugar

Oregano

Parsley

Lavender

Dill

Twenty nails on your hands and feet

Three drops of your blood

A white candle

Fill your bottle halfway with each item, leaving some space for air.

To seal the jar, put a cap on it and drizzle some wax over the top. To safeguard it, bury the bottle in your yard or garden near the front entrance (if you don't have this choice, use the pot of a plant).

5. Spell jar for protection (option 5)

You will need the following ingredients to make this magical bottle to attract protection:

A glass bottle with a stopper of any size

A medallion of St. Michael the Archangel

Powder of olibanum

Myrrh

Palo santo

Laurel *Cinnamon sticks

A piece of iron (any kind)

A piece of copper (any kind)

Seven white candles

Tobacco

Place the components in the bottle (with the medallion at the bottom and the tobacco on top) and allow for some air to escape.

Meanwhile, repeat the following or similar sentences aloud: " "St. Michael the Archangel, noble flora

Please keep the evil away from my home, away from my life, and may your holy soul be with me forever, Thank you, thank you, thank you!" "To seal the jar, pour some wax from one of the candles over the top. Then, cover the jar with a white blanket and set it in a discreet location near your home's entrance.

6. Pet protection spell jar

You will need the following items to construct this magical bottle to protect your favorite pet:

A glass container of any size with a cork

One cup of soil

One cup of sea salt

Bay leaves

Dill seeds

Fennel seeds

Carnelian crystals

A white candle

A pin

Fill the bottom of the bottle with half a cup of soil and the top with half a cup of salt. Then, add the bay leaves, dill, and fennel seeds. Place the second half a cup of salt on top, followed by the other half a cup of earth. Place the carnelian gems above everything.

Allow for some breathing space. Then, lid the jar and drizzle some candle wax over the top to seal it.

Carve "Protect (pet's name)" into the white candle with a pin. Place the candle on top of the jar and burn it whenever you like.

When the light has been out, but the witch bottle is near where your pet spends most of its time.

7. Use a spell jar to keep your house safe.

You will need the following items to produce this magical bottle to attract protection for your home:

Any size glass bottle with a cork

sea salt

cascara powder

labradorite crystals

gold ribbon

blue candle

gold candle

Place the components (excluding the ribbon) into the bottle, leaving some space for air.

Cap the jar and seal it with the wax from the two candles, then wrap the gold ribbon around the bottle.

Bury it in your backyard, garden, or in a plant pot that you'll put on the window nearest to your house's entrance.

8. Use a spell jar to keep your food safe from infection.

You will need the following things to build this magical container to safeguard your food:

Any size glass container with a stopper

Three needles

Three nails

Three pins

Rosemary

Sea salt

A black candle

Fill your bottle halfway with each item, leaving some space for air.

71

Then, lid the jar and drizzle some candle wax over the top to seal it. Shake it nine times forcefully. Then hide it in the kitchen pantry where no one will see it.

9. Protection against Black Magic rituals using a spell jar

You will need the following items to build this magical bottle to protect oneself against any spiritual and energy assaults, as well as Black Magic in general:

Any size glass bottle with a cork

Dried thyme leaves

Dried or fresh rosemary leaves

One lemon peel cut into seven little pieces

Fresh or dried sage leaves

Seven black pepper balls

Seven pine leaves

Seven lavender leaves

Seven bay leaves

One garlic cut into seven small pieces

One tiny strand of the individual whose hair the bottle will protect

Three mistletoe leaves

Three rose thorns

One scarlet ribbon or red wool *

A pen

Apple cider vinegar

A blue candle

A white candle

Three incense sticks of myrrh, sandalwood, rue, laurel, or benzoin (use whatever you have; it may be three of the same or a combination of the ones I specified).

This is certainly one of the most powerful protection spells I've ever heard, and you may use it to protect yourself as well as others.

Before you begin, light a blue and a white candle with your name, as well as the phrases "protection" and "light" written on them.

Allow them to burn.

Before you begin filling the jar, set it aside for a few minutes, perhaps five minutes, between the two candles. Then, layer each component in your bottle, starting with the vinegar and allowing space for air on top.

Before you seal it, hold the jar in your hands and stroll around your home, room by room, envisioning how the bottle captures any bad energy.

Then, place it between the two candles once again. Wait another five minutes before adding some candle wax and incense hashes to the bottle. Then cap it and drizzle a little wax from the two candles (white first, then blue second) over the top to seal it.

Draw a pentagram on the stopper and one at the base of the bottle, then set it between the two candles and keep it there until the candles are consumed.

Then grasp the bottle in your hands and say aloud three times the following or comparable words:

"In the name of Father Sun, Mother Earth, and the Four Elements, I cleanse and eliminate any bad energy from this space.

May physical and energetic protection be maintained, and may peace and harmony prevails in this location.

So it is, and so it shall be."

Place the jar in a hidden location near your front door.

10. A spell jar to keep someone wicked at bay.

You will need the following things to produce this magical bottle to protect yourself from a particularly nasty person:

A glass container of any size with a cork

Cinnamon powder *Black pepper

Red pepper

Hotfoot powder

A tiny paper bag

A black candle

A photo or a little personal item of the nasty person

A black pen

A black ribbon

Using the black ink, write the unpleasant person's name three times horizontally on the paper bag.

"Stay away from me," write three times below. Place the image or personal item inside the bag and secure it with the black ribbon at the bottom of the jar. Place the remaining ingredients in the bottle (hot foot powder on top) and allow some space for air. Please avoid touching your eyes or mouth with these components, especially in this situation!

Meanwhile, recite the following words aloud:

"I beg you, noble elements, to keep evil at bay.

Please allow me to depart in peace and keep (name of the individual) out of my life.

So it is, and so it shall be."

To seal the jar, cap it and drizzle a little candle wax over the top.

After a nine-night vigil, throw this jar into a flowing river or leave it concealed at a crossroads near your home.

Desire and love Spell Jars

11: Love Spell Jar (option 1)

You will need the following items to build this love-attracting magic bottle:

Any size glass container with a cork

A handful of crushed and dried rose petals

Rosemary, dried or fresh

Lavender, dried or fresh

Rose oil or rose water

A pink or red candle

Place the crushed rose petals in the jar. Fill the container halfway with rosemary and lavender, then with rose oil or rose water.

Allow for some breathing space. Then, cap the bottle and drizzle some candle wax over the top to seal it. Put it on a shelf, dresser, or anywhere else in your house where no one will touch it.

12. Love Spell Jar (option 2)

You will need the following items to build this love-attracting magic bottle:

Any size glass bottle with a cork

Honey \sLavander

3 teaspoons Cinnamon Carnation Petals

Rose essential oil

A candle in pink or red

Fill your bottle halfway with each component (with the rose oil on top) and allow some space for air.

Meanwhile, speak the following or comparable phrases aloud:

"Love will arrive; love will no longer keep me waiting."

I believe in the power of herbs and oils; please do it for me, and so be it!"

Cap the bottle and drizzle a little candle wax over the top to seal it. Place it beneath your bed or in the drawer of your nightstand.

13. Attract the person you love with a spell jar

You will need the following things to produce this magical bottle to attract the person you are secretly in love with:

Any size glass bottle with a cork

Five different types of cloves

The oil that lasts forever

Flowers that linger forever

Musk Bee nectar

A ribbon in red

A little paper bag

There are nine red candles.

A photo of the person you want (the smaller, the better)

A red ink pen

Mark all of the candles with the name of the person you love, then rub them with the everlasting oil and save a little amount for your magic jar.

Then, using the red ink, write the name of your love interest nine times horizontally on the paper bag.

Fill in the blanks with your name nine times horizontally, always using the red pen. Place the photo inside the bag and secure it with the red ribbon at the bottom of the jar. Place the remaining ingredients in the bottle (with the honey and eternal oil on top) and allow some space for air.

Meanwhile, speak the following or comparable phrases aloud:

"Species, flowers, herbs, and essential oil"

Please fill their hearts with pleasure, open their eyes, and show them how much they mean to me!

I have faith in you, so be it."

To seal the jar, pour a little wax from one of the candles over the top. For nine days, place the bottle under your bed and recite these words aloud before going to bed.

14. Use a spell jar to find the appropriate person for you.

You will need the following things to produce this magical bottle that will attract the person who is destined for you:

Any size glass bottle with a cork

granulated sugar

The petals of a pink rose

The petals of a red rose

Peeled orange

a slew of pink candies

Powdered cinnamon

A sheet of paper

Pink ink pen

A rose-colored candle

An orange candle

Using a pink pen, write the attributes of the person you want to attract on a sheet of paper. After that, put it at the bottom of your jar.

Add the remaining ingredients (with the petals and cinnamon powder on top), allowing some space for air. Cap the jar and pour some pink candle wax over the top to seal it.

Put it in your backpack and carry it with you at all times to boost your chances of meeting and attracting your other half!

15. Spell jar to attract true love

You will need the following items to produce this magical bottle to finally discover true love:

Linden blossoms of any size, in a glass bottle with a cork

Carnation blossoms

Seeds of coriander

Ginger \sSaffron

Crystals of Amatista

Wine, particularly red wine

A rose-colored candle

Fill the bottle halfway with the ingredients, allowing some space for air.

Cap the jar and pour some pink candle wax over the top to seal it. Hide it in a secure place in your bedroom and hold it in your hands for five minutes every night, concentrating on your purpose.

80

16. Self-love spell jar

You will need the following items to produce this magical bottle to love yourself more:

Any size glass bottle with a cork

shaved sea salt

Powder made from dragon's blood

Crystals of rose quartz

A red cord

A solitary black candle

A rose-colored candle

Fill the bottle halfway with the ingredients, allowing some space for air.

Cap the jar and pour some pink candle wax over the top to seal it. Allow it to burn beside the candles until they are out, then kiss it and charge it with your feelings.

Hide it in a secure place in your bedroom.

17. Use a spell jar to boost sexual desire.

You will need the following items to construct this magical bottle that will help you increase your sexual desire:

Any size glass bottle with a cork

shaved sea salt

Powdered cinnamon

Leaves of Ginkgo biloba

Crystals of ginger goldstone

Wine, particularly red wine

A ribbon in red

A flameless red candle

Place all of the components (except the ribbon) into the bottle (red wine on top), allowing some space for air.

To seal the jar, cap it and drizzle some candle wax over the top.

Then wrap it with the red ribbon.

If you want to boost your sex life with someone, in particular, place a piece of paper at the bottom of the jar with your and your partner's names written on it in red ink. Hide the witch bottle beneath your bed or anywhere else in your bedroom that is secure.

Money, Wealth, and Abundance Jars of Spells

18. Money spell jar (option 1)

You will need the following items to build this money-attracting magic bottle:

Any size glass bottle with a cork

There are five coins.

a single dollar bill

Corn kernels, dried

toasted sesame seeds

Sticks of cinnamon

Cloves of garlic

berries of allspice

Walnuts

A green candle

Fill your bottle halfway with each item, leaving some space for air.

Then, cap the bottle and drizzle some candle wax over the top to seal it. Shake it for five minutes with your dominant hand while repeating this incantation or saying similar things out loud:

"Seeds and silver, corn and barries; please bring me money."

Thank you, thank you, thank you!"

Then, put your witch bottle in a cupboard that no one else can access. Leave your handbag, wallet, or checkbook next to it while you are at home.

19. Money spell jar (option 2)

You will need the following items to build this money-attracting magic bottle:

Any size glass bottle with a cork

Three pieces of money

Oatmeal Corn

Rice

Threads of saffron

Sage

Leaves of laurel

Seeds of cumin

Seeds of dill

A candle in green or yellow

Fill your bottle halfway with each item, leaving some space for air.

Then, lid the jar and drizzle some candle wax over the top to seal it.

Then, hide the witch bottle in your safe or elsewhere in your workplace where no one can discover it.

20. Money spell jar (option 3)

You will need the following items to build this money-attracting magic bottle:

Any size glass bottle with a cork

kosher salt

Glitter in gold

Lentils

Cloves of rice

Sunflower seed oil

Daisy blossoms

Aniseed seeds

The wax from a green or yellow candle

Fill your bottle halfway with each item, leaving some space for air.

Then, lid the jar and drizzle some candle wax over the top to seal it.

Then, hide the witch bottle at the entrance to your home, probably near where you keep your keys and wallet when you get home.

21. Money spell jar (option 4)

You will need the following items to build this money-attracting magic bottle:

Any size glass bottle with a cork

Powdered cinnamon

Honey bees

Crystals of pyrite

A one-dollar banknote

A green candle

A yellow candle

Fill the bottle halfway with the contents (with the dollar bill on the bottom and the crystals on top) and allow some space for air.

Meanwhile, recite aloud the following or similar words: "Noble elements, I trust in you."

Your tremendous energies will bring money and plenty to my household, so be it, and so it will!"

To seal the jar, cap it and drizzle a little wax from the two candles over the top.

Hide it near your altar or in the closet where you store your luggage and money.

22. Money spell jar (option 5)

You will need the following items to build this money-attracting magic bottle:

Any size glass bottle with a cork

There are eight coins.

Thyme dried

Basil, dried

Cloves, ground

1 tablespoon oats

Glitter in gold

A green candle

A yellow candle

A candle made of gold

Fill the bottle halfway with the contents (coins on the bottom, glitter on top), allowing some space for air. Cap the jar and pour some gold candle wax over the top to seal it. It should be left close to the three candles until they are extinguished.

Put it in your bag and bring it to work every day.

23. Spell jar for plenty

You will need the following items to build this abundance-attracting magic bottle:

Any size glass bottle with a cork

Nine coins of varying denominations

Black sand salt

Sugar

Rice

Lentils

Cloves

Leaves of bay

Rue twigs

Savory leaves

Leaves of mint

Sticks of cinnamon

sprigs of rosemary

Three river rocks

A unique silver ring

a ball of yarn

Several pins and nails

Fill your bottle halfway with each item, leaving some space for air.

Meanwhile, say aloud or something close to "Copper and grain, silver and herbs, Please bring me enormous wealth, And so be it!"

Then, hide your witch bottle at the front door or bury it in your garden or backyard.

24. Prosperity spell jar

You will need the following items to build this prosperity-attracting magic bottle:

Any size glass bottle with a cork

Salt

Lentils with gold glitter

Rice

Nutmeg

Cinnamon

Chamomile blossoms

Excellent grass

A coin made of copper

Sunflower seed oil

A candle in green or yellow

A sandalwood sprig

Light your candle and the sandalwood stick together.

Fill your jar with each component, finishing with the sunflower oil and allowing space for air. Cap the bottle and pour some candle wax over the top to seal it.

Meanwhile, speak the following or comparable phrases aloud:

"Copper and grains, herbs, and my hands, please draw unlimited fortune to me, and so be it!"

Allow the candle and incense stick to burn for a few minutes before carefully collecting all of their remnants and burying them, together with your witch bottle, in a plant at home, in your backyard, or a neighboring garden.

25. Prosperity spell jar (option 2)

You will need the following items to build this prosperity-attracting magic bottle:

Any size glass bottle with a cork

shaved sea salt

Allspice

Almonds

Cloves

Prickly pears

Rice

A stale banana

A yellow candle

Fill your bottle halfway with each item, leaving some space for air.

To seal the bottle, pour some of the wax over the top.

Then conceal it in your closet or an office drawer.

26. Health Spell Jars a health spell jar

You will need the following items to build this health-attracting magic bottle:

Any size glass bottle with a cork

kosher salt

Rosemary

White rose petals with basil

Cloves of Laurel

Leaves of Eucalyptus

Seeds of anise

Flower of dandelion

Chamomile flower

A white candle

Fill your bottle halfway with each item, leaving some space for air. Meanwhile, speak the following or comparable phrases aloud:

"Salt, leaves, herbs, flowers, and grains, Your power is tremendous, your power is excellent, Protect my health, and I shall be eternally grateful!"

Then, lid the jar and drizzle a little candle wax over the top to seal it.

Place it next to your bed or next to the bed of the person whose health you want to protect.

27. Health Spell Jar (option 2)

You'll need the following items to produce this magical bottle to assist you to take care of your health:

Any size glass bottle with a cork

shaved sea salt

Petals from sunflowers

Leaves of Eucalyptus

Dill \sFennell

sprigs of caraway

Crystals of clear quartz

A green candle

28. Fertility spell jar

You will need the following items to prepare this magical bottle that will not only help you conceive but will also safeguard your pregnancy:

Any size glass bottle with a cork

shaved sea salt

Geranium

Prickly pears

Sage

Crystals of red jade

A green candle

Fill the bottle halfway with the ingredients, allowing some space for air. Meanwhile, speak the following or similar lines aloud: " "I yearn for you with all my heart, and I wait for you with open arms.

Come to me, and so it will be!"

To seal the jar, cap it and drizzle a little candle wax over the top.

Hide the witch bottle under your bed or someplace else in your bedroom.

Repeat the spell's phrases every night if you want to boost the jar's potency.

29. Anti-depression spell jar

You will need the following items to produce this magical bottle to help you deal with sadness and feel more pleased and upbeat:

Any size glass bottle with a cork

shaved sea salt

Marjoram

Passionflower

Leaves of Ginkgo Biloba

Crystals of Carnelian

Crystals of smoky quartz

Crystals of lepidolite

An orange candle

Fill the bottle halfway with the ingredients, allowing some space for air.

To seal the jar, cap it and drizzle some candle wax over the top.

Put it in your luggage and carry it with you everywhere you go to help you deal with your emotions.

30. Anxiety-relieving spell jar

You will need the following items to prepare this magical bottle that will help you reduce your anxiety and feel more peaceful and relaxed:

Any size glass bottle with a cork

shaved sea salt

Crystals of jasper

Crystals of obsidian

Crystals with angel auras

Chamomile \sLavender

A white candle

Fill the bottle halfway with the ingredients, allowing some space for air.

To seal the jar, cap it and drizzle some candle wax over the top.

Put it in your luggage and carry it with you everywhere you go to help you deal with your emotions.

31. Psychic powers spell jar

You'll need the following items to produce this magical bottle to boost your psychic abilities:

Any size glass bottle with a cork

Cinnamon

Nutmeg

Allspice

Ginger

Basil

Seeds of fennel

Garlic

Sage marjoram

Cloves of garlic

The mustard seed

A white candle

Fill your bottle halfway with each item, leaving some space for air.

Then, lid the jar and drizzle some candle wax over the top to seal it. Then, breath deeply, gently shake the container and recite aloud the following or similar words: " "Please help me, magic herbs.

Improve my psychic talents, and so it will be." "

Bury it in a remote section of your garden, yard, or accessible ground near your home. Then, above it, draw a pentagram (a five-pointed star).

32. Use a spell jar to improve the household atmosphere and prevent arguments.

To create this magical bottle, which is ideal for fighting families, you will need the following ingredients:

Any size glass bottle with a cork

Chamomile

Basil

Peppermint

Honey bees

A ribbon in red

Some of the hair from several family members

A little paper bag

There are seven pink candles.

Take a paper bag and write the names of the family members three times horizontally, followed by the words "Harmony" and "Peace" three times below. Place the hair in the bag and close it with the red ribbon at the bottom of the jar.

Place the remaining ingredients in the bottle (with honey on top) and allow for some air to escape.

Meanwhile, speak the following or similar lines aloud: " "Hamomile, use your power to soothe the harshness and prevent jealousy among these individuals; Basil, scent their hearts and bring them success and plenty; and Peppermint, provide them peace and harmony, love, and protection.

That's OK."

To seal the jar, pour a little wax from one of the candles over the top. Place the bottle someplace in the family room or kitchen that is not visible. Soon, you will notice how the home will regain its equilibrium.

33. Use a spell jar to soften an aggressive individual.

You will need the following items to prepare this magical bottle to regulate the aggression of someone who has a bad temper:

Any size glass bottle with a cork

Chamomile

Powdered cinnamon

Petals of a sandpaper vine

Honey bees

A ribbon in red

A little paper bag

Three pink pillar candles

A depiction of the aggressive individual (the smaller, the better)

a dark pen

A red ink pen

Using the black ink, write the name of the bad-tempered individual nine times horizontally on the paper bag. Using the red pen, write your name nine times horizontally below. Place the photo inside the bag and secure it with the red ribbon at the bottom of the jar. Fill the bottle halfway with the remaining ingredients (honey on top) and allow some space for air.

Meanwhile, recite the following or similar sentences aloud: " "Please soothe their rage, Cinnamon, sweeten their heart and bring them love, Sandpaper vine, tame their heart and make them as docile as a tiny lamb.

Now that their names are permanently linked, may they live in peace, harmony, and togetherness?" "

To seal the jar, pour a little wax from one of the candles over the top. Place the bottle someplace concealed near the individual who is being abusive to you. Soon, you will see that people will begin to treat you with education and respect.

34. A Goddess-honoring Spell Jar

You will need the following items to construct this magical bottle to respect and seek protection from the Deity of your choice:

Any size glass bottle with a cork

A stone discovered in a park

Seven bobby pins

thirty-one corn kernels

a smidge

7 tbsp. honey from bees

The oil that lasts forever

Sacred water

A yellow candle

Fill the bottle halfway with the components (honey, oil, wine, and holy water on top) and allow some space for air. To seal the jar, cap it and drizzle some candle wax over the top. Then, cover it with a yellow cloth and set it near a window for three days, where it will be exposed to direct sunshine. After some time has gone, remove the yellow cloth and put your magic jar in a hidden location at your house's entrance or near your altar.

35. Good luck charm jar

You will need the following things to build this good luck magic bottle:

Any size glass bottle with a cork

Chamomile

granulated sugar

Cinnamon

Crystals of amethyst

Crystals of aventurine

Crystals of jasper

The bay leaf

Seeds of star aniseSacred water

Three green candlesticks

On your bay leaf, write the words "I'm fortunate." Then, using tweezers, place the leaf on the flame of the middle candle to send your message to the Universe and record its hashes.

Place the ingredients in the bottle (hashes and holy water on top) and allow some space for air. To seal the jar, pour a little wax from one of the candles over the top.

Hide it someplace secure near the front door to bring good fortune for you and your whole family.

36. Use a spell jar to wish someone special luck.

You will need the following things to construct this magical bottle to bring good luck to a loved one:

Any size glass bottle with a cork

Seeds of cumin

Leaves of ash

Nutmeg

Vanilla bean pods

Crystals of jasper

A bag made of paper

The individual's image (the smaller, the better)

A white candle

Put a photograph of the person you want to wish luck to in a paper bag and place it at the bottom of the jar. Then, within the bottle, combine the remaining components, leaving some space for air. To seal the bottle, cap it and drizzle a little candle wax over the top.

Hide it someplace near to the person's residence (the closer, the better) to allow the good luck energies to reach their location.

37. White Magic Attraction Spell Jar

You will need the following things to build this magical bottle that will draw all the magical forces and energy around you:

Any size glass bottle with a cork

shaved sea salt

granulated sugar

Crystals of clear quartz

 berries of juniper

Leaves of basil

Powdered angelica root

Three purple pillar candles

Fill the bottle halfway with the ingredients, allowing some space for air.

To seal the jar, pour a little wax from one of the candles over the top. Keep it close to the candles until they are out.

Place it in a hidden location near your altar to boost the potency of your rituals, or take it with you in your purse to draw magical energies everywhere you go!

38. Spell jar to help you stop a bad habit

To create this magical bottle to stop a bad habit that you can't seem to shake, you'll need the following ingredients:

Any size glass bottle with a cork

shaved sea salt

Dargon's Catnip blood incense

An onion, dried

A little paper bag

A strand of your hair

A dark pen

A single black candle

Write the bad behavior you want to break on the paper bag with the black ink, then place the hair lock inside and seal it with the black ribbon. Place it in the bottom of the bottle and fill it with the remaining ingredients, leaving space for some air.

Cap the bottle and pour some candle wax over the top to seal it.

Place it in a hidden location in the room that is most closely associated with your undesirable behavior. If you can't stop eating junk food, for example, conceal your jar in the kitchen pantry.

39. Spell jar for safe travel

To build this magical bottle that will protect you and keep you safe while traveling to any place, you will need the following ingredients:

Any size glass bottle with a cork

Rosemary \sRue

103

Comfrey root basil

Crystals of garnet

Crystals of moonstone

A solitary black candle

Fill the bottle halfway with the ingredients, allowing some space for air.

Meanwhile, recite the following or similar sentences aloud: " "hunters, hail, and snow will not halt my progress,

I'll go safe and sound, and I'll have a great time!" "

To seal the jar, cap it and drizzle a little candle wax over the top.

Put it in your luggage or baggage before heading off on your next journey!

40. Negativity-repelling spell jar

You will need the following items to build this magical bottle to ward against bad energies:

Any size glass bottle with a cork

Sacred water

Basil leaves, fresh

Mint leaves

Powdered cinnamon

Petals of violet

a slew of thumbtacks

A little scrap of paper and a black pen

A solitary black candle

A flameless red candle

Using the black ink, write your name on the sheet of paper. After that, put it at the bottom of your jar.

Add the remaining ingredients (with the petals and blessed water on top), allowing some space for air. Cap the jar and pour some black candle wax over the top to seal it.

Place it someplace inconspicuous near your front door, or bury it in your garden or backyard.

41. Spell jar to start again and leave the past in the past

You will need the following items to produce this magical bottle for fresh beginnings:

Any size glass bottle with a cork

shaved sea salt

Rosemary

Powdered cinnamon

Cloves, whole

Crystals of rainbow moonstone

Crystals of Amazonite

A little scrap of paper and a black pen

A white candle

Using the black ink, write on the sheet of paper the things you want to leave behind you and your aspirations for the future. After that, put it at the bottom of your jar. Add the other ingredients (with the cinnamon powder on top), allowing some space for air. To seal the jar, cap it and drizzle some white candle wax over the top.

Hide it in the room that best depicts the things you wish to leave behind or that best matches your new beginning.

42. Conjure courage with a spell jar

You will need the following things to construct this magical bottle to enhance your courage:

Any size glass bottle with a cork

shaved sea salt

Lavender

An anise seed pod

Rosemary

a metal piece

Crystals of sunstone

1 tablespoon vodka

An orange candle

Fill the bottle halfway with the ingredients (vodka on top), allowing some space for air. To seal the jar, cap it and drizzle some candle wax over the top.

Put it in your luggage and take it with you to any location or "task" that needs an additional dosage of daring.

43. Spell jar with the Four Elements to guard against harmful forces

You will need the following items to build this magical bottle to defend yourself with the power of the Four Elements:

Any size glass bottle with a cork

shaved sea salt (representing Earth)

A black thread

A minuscule mirror

seashells, crushed (representing Water)

Dried basil ashes (representing Fire)

Sage in white (representing Air)

A solitary black candle

Place all of the contents (save the rope) into the bottle, allowing some space for air.

Meanwhile, recite the following aloud: " "the elements of fire, air, earth, and water,

107

I turn to heavenly elements, keep me secure, keep the devil at bay, I trust divine elements in you, thank you!" "

To seal the jar, cap it and drizzle a little candle wax over the top.

After that, wrap the thread around it.

Place it someplace secure at the front door of your home.

44. Spell jar to increase your Four Elements Magic

You will need the following items to build this magical bottle to be a better witch due to the power of the Four Elements:

Any size glass bottle with a cork

shaved sea salt

The soil (representing Earth) is a slew of stones

Driftwood (representing Water)

An orange candle's wax (representing Fire)

You discovered a feather on the street (representing Air)

* An orange candle

Fill the bottle halfway with the ingredients, allowing some space for air.

To seal the jar, cap it and drizzle some candle wax over the top.

Hide it in your closet and bring it out to put it on your altar whenever you are practicing a spell that requires the power of the Four Elements: having this jar is like having an extra boost in this way to me.

45. Spell jar to ward off ill-luck

You will need the following items to build this magical bottle to protect you from whoever is giving you negative energies:

Any size glass bottle with a cork

Dill with sea salt

Pins of any type

A ribbon in black

Wine, particularly red wine

A solitary black candle

Place the ingredients in the bottle (red wine on top), allowing some space for air. To seal the jar, cap it and drizzle some candle wax over the top.

Bury the bottle as far away from your home as possible so that it can keep ill-luck at bay.

46. Happiness Spell Jar

You will need the following items to produce this mood-boosting magic bottle:

Any size glass bottle with a cork

shaved sea salt

Shavings of cedar

Petals of marigold

109

Peeled orange

Savory

Oregano

Crystals of black tourmaline

A yellow candle

Fill the bottle halfway with the ingredients, allowing some space for air.

To seal the jar, cap it and drizzle some candle wax over the top.

Hide the bottle in the room where you spend most of your time, or keep it in your luggage so you can carry it with you everywhere you go.

47. Use a spell jar to boost your inventiveness.

You will need the following things to construct this magical bottle that will inspire you to be more creative:

Any size glass bottle with a cork

shaved sea salt

Peppermint

Rosemary

Sage

Roots of ginseng

Crystals of citrine

A candle in purple

Fill the bottle halfway with the ingredients, allowing some space for air.

To seal the jar, cap it and drizzle some candle wax over the top.

Hide the bottle in a drawer of your desk, whether at home or work or carry it with you to attract fresh ideas and inspiration everywhere you go.

48. Mental fortitude spell jar

You will need the following things to construct this magical bottle that will help you feel more confident and mentally stronger:

Any size glass bottle with a cork

shaved sea salt

Crystals of citrine

Crystals of aventurine

Crystals of Tiger's Eye

Sage

Peppermint Rosemary

An orange candle

Fill the bottle halfway with the ingredients, allowing some space for air.

111

To seal the jar, cap it and drizzle some candle wax over the top.

Hide it in the room of the home where you spend the most time. Otherwise, keep it in your backpack and bring it with you when you know you'll be confronted with a particularly difficult scenario or one that will need a lot of mental fortitude.

49. Peace spell jar

You will need the following things to build this magic bottle to assist you to cultivate a tranquil atmosphere around you:

Any size glass bottle with a cork

shaved sea salt

Basil Lemongrass

Catnip

Branches of olive

Petals of violet

Crystals of citrine

A white candle

A piece of white ribbon

Fill the bottle halfway with the ingredients, allowing some space for air.

To seal the jar, cap it and drizzle some candle wax over the top.

Tie the white ribbon around the jar to strengthen your purpose. Hide it in the room of the home where your family spends the most time together.

Jars of Chakra Spells

Our physical body is surrounded by an unseen energy field known as the aura, as you are surely aware.

The aura has seven energy centers called chakras. They are spinning rings of subtle energy in the form of a funnel that runs down the spine. They absorb higher abilities and turn them into a form that may be used by the physical body.

They are continually evolving, as their name indicates (chakra is Sanskrit for "wheel"). The chakras may attract and release energy as a result of this spinning.

The chakras are associated with the bodily processes of excretion, reproduction, digestion, circulation, breathing, and the central nervous system. However, they also link to our emotional and spiritual systems, which is why the status of our chakras may read our feelings and attitude toward life.

The seven chakras are as follows:

Root or Base Chakra: This chakra is situated at the base of the spin and is considered the body's survival center. It has a red color frequency.

Sacral Chakra: This chakra is located in the lower belly or pelvic area and is considered the body's emotional center.

It has an orange color frequency.

113

Solar Plexus Chakra: This chakra is situated in the belly and is known as the body's power center. It has a yellow color frequency.

Heart Chakra: Located in the chest, it is known as the Relationship Center of the body. It has a green color frequency.

Throat Chakra: This chakra is located in the throat, neck, thyroid, and jaw and is known as the body's communication center. It has a blue color frequency.

Third Eye Chakra: This chakra is located in the area between the eyes and is known as the body's intuition center. It has an indigo color frequency.

Crown Chakra: Located at the top of the head, it is considered the body's Enlightenment Center. It has a violet color frequency.

The particular bottles listed below provide a beautiful and effective method to concentrate on your objectives and balance each of your chakras. Their components, of course, take into mind the precise correspondences of each chakra. They may provide even more advantages when infused with Reiki.

50. Root Chakra Jar.

You will need the following items to prepare this magical bottle to promote grounding and stability and repair your root chakra:

Any size glass bottle with a cork

shaved sea salt

Crystals of hematite

Carnelian red crystals

Crystals of bloodstone

Cedarwood essential oil

Leaves of beetroot

chile pepper

Sage in white

A flameless red candle

Fill the bottle halfway with the ingredients, allowing some space for air.

To seal the jar, cap it and drizzle some candle wax over the top.

For 10 minutes, imagine a red light rotating and shining while breathing regularly. Place the bottle in an out-of-the-way location in your home.

51. Sacral Chakra Jar

You will need the following items to prepare this magical bottle to improve security and creativity while also healing your sacral chakra:

Any size glass bottle with a cork

shaved sea salt

Crystals of moonstone

Crystals of dark amber

Crystals of Tiger's Eye

Sandalwood essential oil

Peeled orange

powdered dahlia

An orange candle

Fill the bottle halfway with the ingredients, allowing some space for air.

To seal the jar, cap it and drizzle a little candle wax over the top.

For 10 minutes, imagine an orange light shining and pulsating to the beat of your breath. Place the bottle in an out-of-the-way location in your home.

52. Solar Plexus Chakra jar

You will need the following items to prepare this magical bottle to raise your confidence and cure your solar plexus chakra:

Any size glass bottle with a cork

shaved sea salt

Crystals of citrine

Agata crystals of light

Crystals of calcite

Clove essential oil

Lemongrass

Ginger

A yellow candle

Fill the bottle halfway with the ingredients, allowing some space for air.

To seal the jar, cap it and drizzle some candle wax over the top.

For 10 minutes, imagine a yellow light flashing and pulsating to the beat of your breath. Place the bottle in an out-of-the-way location in your home.

53. Heart Chakra Jar.

You will need the following things to produce this magical bottle to provide love to yourself and others while also healing your heart chakra:

Any size glass bottle with a cork

shaved sea salt

Crystals of jade

Crystals of rose quartz

Crystals of malachite

Lavender essential oil

Jasmine

Petals of roses

A green candle

Fill the bottle halfway with the ingredients, allowing some space for air.

To seal the jar, cap it and drizzle some candle wax over the top.

For 10 minutes, imagine a bright green light blazing and beating as you inhale and exhale. Place the bottle in an out-of-the-way location in your home.

54. Jar of the Throat Chakra

You will need the following items to prepare this magical bottle that will enhance your communication, help you speak the truth, and heal your throat chakra:

Any size glass bottle with a cork

shaved sea salt

Crystals of apatite

Crystals of turquoise

Crystals of aquamarine

Bergamot essential oil

Sage

Chamomile

A blue candle

Fill the bottle halfway with the ingredients, allowing some space for air.

To seal the jar, cap it and drizzle some candle wax over the top.

For 10 minutes, imagine a deep blue light shining and moving in time with your breath. Place the bottle in an out-of-the-way location in your home.

55. Jar for the Third Eye Chakra

You will need the following items to prepare this magical bottle to boost your intuition, connect with the Universe, and heal your third eye chakra:

Any size glass bottle with a cork

shaved sea salt

Crystals of azurite

Crystals of calcite

Crystals of sodalite

Mint essential oil

Passionflower \sSandalwood

A candle made of indigo

Fill the bottle halfway with the ingredients, allowing some space for air.

To seal the jar, cap it and drizzle some candle wax over the top.

119

For 10 minutes, imagine a brilliant azure light shining and beating as you breathe in and out. Place the bottle in an out-of-the-way location in your home.

56. Crown Chakra jar

You will need the following things to produce this magical bottle to boost your spiritual connections and repair your head chakra:

Any size glass bottle with a cork

shaved sea salt

Crystals of howlite

Crystals of sugilite

Crystals of Alexandrite

Myrrh essential oil

Lavander

a candle in violet

Fill the bottle halfway with the ingredients, allowing some space for air.

To seal the jar, cap it and drizzle some candle wax over the top.

For 10 minutes, imagine a dazzling violet light shining and moving in time with your breath. Place the bottle in an out-of-the-way location in your home.